MW00513738

A Letter From Lieut. Gen. Burgoyne to his Constituents, Upon his Late Resignation; With the Correspondences Between the Secretaries of War and him, Relative to his Return to America. The Third Edition

A

LETTER

FROM

LIEUT. GEN. BURGOYNE

TO HIS

CONSTITUENTS,

UPON HIS LATE

RESIGNATION;

WITH THE

CORRESPONDENCES

BETWEEN THE

SECRETARIES OF WAR
AND HIM,

RELATIVE TO

HIS RETURN TO AMERICA.

THE THIRD EDITION

LONDON·

PRINTED FOR J ALMON, OPPOSITE BURLINGTON-HOUSE,
PICCADILLY. MDCCLXXIX.

*To the Gentlemen, Clergy, and other Voters of the
Town of Preston.*

GENTLEMEN,

THE refponfibility for political conduct,
and perhaps for all conduct, which every
Reprefentative owes in a certain degree to the
nation at large, and particularly owes to his
immediate Conftituents, becomes a more forci-
ble duty upon me from the many private friendfhips with which I am honoured among you.

The crifis in which I write is another reafon
for this addrefs. Never, furely, was there a
time in which it was fo important for Confti-
tuent and Reprefentative to underftand each
other; nor ever was there one when more
fyftematic pains were taken to fet them at va-
riance.

My firft purpofe is to explain to you the
caufes which have induced me to withdraw
myfelf from a ftation, in which (till it is
known that my offers of fervice were rejected)
I might be fuppofed capable of ferving my
country in her extremity with fome effect.
Thefe caufes fhall be ftated faithfully. It is
the intereft and pride of the innocent and in-
jured to be ingenuous.

B   For

For the better underſtanding my caſe, it may be neceſſary to take a ſhort retroſpect of ſome of the leading principles and ſituations by which I have been governed.

I had been a member of the Houſe of Commons nearly an entire Parliament before I became a candidate for Preſton. The teſtimony of my conduct during that time, of which I was moſt proud, was the approbation of Lord Strange, under whoſe auſpicies I firſt offered myſelf to your favour. It was my happineſs to be his relation; but it was my higheſt honour that he was my friend by choice. You knew him well—His natural affections were ſtrong, but his public virtues were inflexible; and no family connection or intereſt, unaccompanied with opinion, could have influenced his recommendation for a truſt from the people.

The ſyſtem upon which I had acted the preceding Parliament, and upon which I continued to act in the ſeat your favour gave me, was ſhort and plain;—a conſtitutional ſupport of the Crown—a liberal reliance on thoſe who then conducted the public meaſures—but an independent claim to free opinion and free conduct upon every occaſion in which my judgment called upon me to depart from my general line.

Government gave me countenance and gave me favours; but never at the expence of thoſe principles· and I reflect with pleaſure and

gratitude

gratitude on the fanction you have given, Gentlemen, to this affertion, by having, after thofe favours from the Crown, elected me with uncommon marks of your approbation.

Conformable to the principles I have ftated, notwithftanding my general fupport of adminiftration, I had found myfelf obliged fometimes to oppofe the meafures of the Court ; particularly in the debates upon the Convention relative to Falkland's Ifland ; upon the proceedings relative to the Caribbees ; and upon the perpetuity of Mr. Grenville's bill. In the motion I made for the committee of enquiry into the ftate of the India Companv, and through the whole progrefs of that long bufinefs, I acted without the participation of the Minifters ; and fuch accidents of feparation had arifen between Lord North (the fuppofed leading Minifter) and me, that, although I bore refpect to his character, no two perfons, not in direct enmity, could live at a greater diftance. Such was my political fituation when I was called to the American fervice in the year 1775.

It is known to thofe who employed me, and I have often declared it in public, that I was involuntarily called to it. I was not without profeffional reafons for wifhing to decline it ; but I had many others, arifing from fuch perfonal circumftances as moft naturally and ftrongly affect the human mind—They are not unknown to you.

I ftated

I ftated thefe fentiments when the King's intention of employing me was communicated, adding, that powerful as they were, they fhould be made fubfervient to the principles I had ever held of a foldier's duty ; and if his Majefty thought me, then the laft and humbleft upon the lift of his major-generals, to be neceffary to the fervice of the ftate, I fhould forego any idea of excufing myfelf upon the plea of my private circumftances. I was affured, in terms very honourable to me, that his Majefty was decided in his choice of generals, and I immediately declared my readinefs to obey

Thus engaged, I refolved to dedicate myfelf to my new fituation. I faw the national objects to which it opened. I had uniformly fupported the principle then held out by the Min fters—the fupremacy of the King in Parliament ; and from truly public fenfations, I endeavoured to put myfelf upon as good terms as poffible with the Firft Lord of the Treafury I fuggefted a command at New-York with four regiments (it was the very beginning of the troubles) with a view to negotiation, not to arms. The idea feemed to be much approved ; but I am not mafter of the fecret and political circumftances that prevented its being adopted. I am now inclined to believe that had the meafure taken place, the war would have been prevented ; or at leaft

it

it would have begun with that important place being in the King's government.

In the courfe of the enfuing campaign (if the blockade of Bofton can be called by that name) my efforts to be of ufe in the public fervice were not confined to the immediate line of my ftation, but were exerted at large, and received very flattering teftimonies of approbation at home and abroad.

Late in the winter of 1775 I returned to England. The King's Minifters faw and acknowledged, that in the reafons for that return, my zeal for the public fervice kept pace with the anxieties of my private fituation. It entirely prevailed over them, when very early in the fpring I was called upon for fervice in Canada. It may be fuppofed that I folicited that deftination (as by fome it was fuppofed that I had folicited the former one). The contrary was fo true, that I would have purchafed a redemption from the fervice, would my principle of public honour have permitted, with the laft fhilling of my military income. At the time I embarked, acute diftemper was added to pain of mind, arifing from the family diftrefs I before alluded to, and the circumftances requiring my continuance in England were become much more affecting than the year before.

My endeavours in the campaign under Sir Guy Carleton, in 1776, were alfo thought worthy commendation ; and before my return

turn I was pitched upon for the command of the troops deftined to make a junction with Sir William Howe from Canada.

I had now fuftained the fevere private misfortune which I had fo long dreaded Employment in the field was the beft relief that could be offered to affliction; and for the firft time fince the war I was earneft to go to America.

I have flightly touched this progrefs of my late fervice, to fhew that the fituation in which I was placed in the year 1777, was not one of private favour, court intrigue, or perfonal ambition, but naturally devolving to me from occurrences and from general opinion. Whether that opinion was juftly founded, this is not the place to difcufs. An account of the campaign, in the part where I commanded, will forthwith be fubmitted to the public in a detail of the facts proved before Parliament, and in other authentic documents. In the mean time let me be permitted to fay, that however freely cavillers and fpeculatifts may have treated my military conduct, none have difputed the principle and zeal which actuated my endeavours.

With thofe claims, Gentlemen, to the countenance and good-will at leaft of government, I proceed to relate the treatment I received.

I had expreffed, in my private letter from Albany to the Secretary of State, my " con-
" fidence in the juftice of the King and his
" Councils to fupport the General they had
" thought

" thought proper to appoint to as arduous an
" undertaking and under as positive a direc-
" tion as a cabinet ever framed." I had in the
same letter given an opinion of the enemy's
troops, upon near inspection of their numbers,
appointment and discipline.

Furnished with these materials, and sup-
ported by the fidelity with which I had acted,
it was not thought expedient I should have
access to the King. What other facts might
have been cleared up by my interview, and
were wished not to be cleared up, the Secretary of State* only can inform the world. Direct means of effecting my exclusion from the
King's presence were not practicable; for the
case was unprecedented. The pretext adopted
was as follows.

It was suggested that an enquiry should be
made by a board of General Officers into the
causes of the miscarriage of the Northern Expedition; and a court *etiquette* was invented,
the foundation of which in reason or precedent I am not acquainted with, *viz.* that
the persons whose conduct was so put in
question, should not appear at Court pending
the enquiry. No difficulty of the competency
of such a court was then spoke of, or perhaps

---

* Whenever *the Secretary of State* is mentioned in these
papers, the person to be understood is the Secretary for
the American department, Lord George Germain.

thought

thought of, by any but the dark defigners of my ruin; the meafure therefore could neither affect his Majefty nor his Court with any idea of farther hardfhip than the delay of a few days to my appearing in his prefence.

This arrangement had been prepared by the Secretary of State, in the interval between the notice of my arrival at Portfmouth, which he received in the evening, and my vifit to him in Pall-Mall, which was before noon the next day.

It will naturally be fuppofed that the ftate in which I ftood was the firft fubject of converfation; on the contrary, I was received with much apparent kindnefs; explanations paffed, but they were friendly; I was heard attentively, through a report of all the tranfactions fubfequent to the Convention of Saratoga, and I was led by degrees, and without fufpicion of infidioufnefs, to the moft confidential communication, on my part, of facts, obfervations, and opinions, refpecting very important objects.

If the meafure of denying me accefs to the King had been undecided before, this converfation was of a nature to produce a decifion; for it opened truths refpecting the difpofitions of the people of America, and the ftate of things there, very different from the ideas which (it is now known, from the line taken by the Secretary of State in the late enquiry) were prevalent in the governing Councils of this kingdom.

It

It was not 'till after the matter of my communication was exhaufted, that the Secretary of State drew from his pocket an order, that I fhould prepare myfelf for an enquiry : at which I expreffed my fulleft fatisfaction, till he followed the order with the information of the *etiquette* I before mentioned, that I was not to appear at Court.

Having pitched upon this expedient for no other end than to exclude me from the prefence of my Sovereign, he could hardly be in pain about the event. If the General Officers appointed for a Board of Enquiry, fhould coincide with the notion that my parole was of fuch a nature as to bar their proceedings, this would put off my accefs to the King to a very long day : but if the General Officers fhould not enter into thefe ideas, he had a refource left. He could not be unapprized, that fuch a court was held by high authorities in the law to be illegal ; and if I was not to fee the King until an illegal or queftionable court fhould make a valid report, I was never likely to enjoy that honour. Either way I was not to have the benefit of an Enquiry ; but he was to have the advantage of the *pretence* of one, in order to fhut the door of St. James's againft me. This has been made apparent beyond all poffibility of doubt, by every part of his fubfequent conduct : but at that time, though I faw a difgrace was intended me, I was not able to eftimate the full extent of it.

C

Thus

Thus prevented in my intended appeal to the King, and as I have fatal reason to believe, the King's ear secured against me, attempts were not unthought of to deprive me of a voice in Parliament. A great Law Officer of the Crown, made, *in the form of* legal doubts, a long and methodical argument against my competence to any civil duty or function : but it was not found so easy to exclude me from your service, as it had been to deprive me of countenance at Court ; and ministers only shewed by that abortive attempt, what their motives were, in those attempts in which they had been more successful.

Though the late time of the session, and the absence of Sir William Howe and Sir Guy Carleton, who were supposed to be parties, furnished plausible arguments for postponing a Parliamentary Enquiry in the summer of 1778, it was evident the temper of the House of Commons was inclined to adopt it at the ensuing meeting.

In the beginning of June, I received the conditional order annexed. [*App. No.* 1.] Tho' it bears the King's name, it was avowedly a Letter of the Cabinet: and there remained no longer a doubt in my mind, that my ruin was made a measure of state. Few adepts in the science of oppression could have formed a design better fitted to its end ; and it was likely to be successful, whatever part I should take. If I went—my character was lost irretrievably—the falshoods and aspersions that have since been

refuted

refuted in the face of thofe who propagated them, were already gone forth : the numbers of my army, and of that oppofed to me, were already grofsly miftated ; contradictory charges of floth and precipitancy, as the temper of men at the moment feemed inclined to either, were fupported with uniform perfeverance :— my friends were ftated to be my accufers ; and even my integrity, with regard to pecuniary trufts, was glanced at.

If I ftayed, the King's order (as it was fallacioufly called) was a fpecious topick ; and it was not difficult to forefee, that it would be put into the hands of gentlemen that well knew how to make the utmoft of it by art and opportunity. My anfwer [*App. No.* 2.] drew from the cabinet their fecond letter [*App. No.* 3] and I give them the fatisfaction of knowing, that I felt all they could wifh I fhould feel from the repetition of their feverity. I faw in it at once a doubt of my veracity refpecting my health, and the moft contemptuous difregard of all other principles upon which I had claimed a right of ftaying in this country.—Fundamental principles, I thought them, of juftice and generofity due from all governments to thofe who ferve them zealoufly, and in fome governments held doubly due to fuch as in their zeal have been unfortunate.

It muft be obferved, that the miniftry kept a profound filence, both to myfelf and the public, refpecting the ratification of the convention.

C 2

tion. The same silence they maintained even in Parliament long after its meeting. They were perfectly apprifed, that the enemy had some time before made the want of that ratification the ground of their refusing to give effect to the part of the treaty which was favourable to the troops. They knew also, that one of the principal objects of my return to England was to negotiate in behalf of that deferving body of foldiers and subjects. Their defire of my delivering myself into captivity, at such a time, and under such circumstances, justified something more than a suspicion, that in my absence in was intended either to lay to my charge some breach of faith with the enemy; or to renounce the treaty from the beginning; and by my surrender, to transfer the act from the nation to my person. These are the only two cases which I believe can be produced from the history of nations. wherein an officer, who had made a convention with an enemy, had been delivered up to them. The ratification of the treaty afterwards is no proof that such intentions did not then exift.

I will make no farther obfervations, gentlemen, upon this first correfpondence between the War-Office and me; nor should I have troubled you with thefe, but that great pains are taken to divert the attention of the public from the pretended order, to my behaviour fince the receipt of it. I in no wife feek to evade the public judgment upon any thing I have done: but I claim from the impartial and

the

the candid, a confideration of the pretended order itfelf, in its principal parts, *viz* the ground
upon which it is founded; the novel fpecies of
cruelty which it fuppofes within the power of
the Crown; and laftly, the exercife of fuch
doctrine by men who were parties, and againft
the man whom they were called upon by their
ftation and their honour to confront.

Nothing farther paffed during the recefs of
Parliament. I availed myfelf of a difcretio-
nary power, as I had a right to do, and I made
it no fecret, that had a direct order been fent
me, I fhould have laid all my commiffions at
his Majefty's feet.

During the laft feffion of Parliament, an
enquiry was inftituted. The detail of the attempts made by the Miniftry to defeat it, is
too notorious to be neceffary upon this occafion. They at laft contrived, that it fhould
be left imperfect: but in fpight of every ma-
nagement, it had anfwered my purpofe fo far,
as to fix upon record a body of evidence, that
I would not exchange for all that power could
beftow. It is a juftification of misfortune by
the voice of Honour. It is there apparent,
what the army under my command, who felt
moft and faw beft, thought of my actions.
—The affections of my gallant comrades, un-
fhaken in every trial, labour, famine, captivity, or death, enable me to defpife the rancour
of a cabal and all its confequences.

The moft important purpofe of my return
to England having been anfwered by this
vin-

vindication, I thought the facrifice of my commiffions, the fruits of the greateft part of my
life, not to be neceffary. I knew by experience, what I had to apprehend in point of
health from an American winter, but I fcorn-
ed to plead it. Confcious of my integrity, I
abandoned my public accounts to the rigorous
fcrutiny of office; and I took occafion publicly
to declare, that fhould it ftill be thought expedient to deliver me back to the enemy, and a
pofitive order fhould be fent me for that purpofe, I fhould, as far as in me lay, obey it.

I do not believe any man who knows me
doubted the fincerity of that intention. I am
perfuaded, the framers of the letter of the 24th
September were particularly convinced of it.
The man who embarked in the fituation I did,
in the year 1776, could hardly be fuppofed to
want fortitude to undertake an American voy-
age, in the fituation in which I made the declaration. An order, therefore, which I could
have obeyed without committing my honour,
would not have effected my ruin. Time and
circumftances furnifhed more fecure expedients;
which I fhall now open.

Occafions were taken to vifit my offences
upon my friends. Examples refpecting my
neareft connections need not be pointed out,
when I am addreffing myfelf to any part of
the county of Lancafter. But the principle
extended far more wide; and did not the ap-
prehenfion of farther hurting the men I love

reftrain

reſtrain me, I could produce inſtances of hard-
ſhip in the diſtribution of military preferments,
that no impartial perſon will impute to any
other cauſe than the kindneſs and friendſhip of
the parties to me.

These inſtances of perſecution, it was well
known, affected me deeply. There were others
yet more irritating.

In the courſe of the ſummer, the apprehen-
ſions before entertained of an invaſion, by the
declaration of government, became a certain-
ty. Hardly a Britiſh ſubject could be found
ſo low, ſo feeble, or even ſo profligate, as to
be exempted from ſervice; while uncommon
premiums were raiſed by begging, and diſtri-
buted to volunteers, the goals, and even the
feet of the gallows, were reſorted to for other
recruits.

In this declared dilemma, I know government were not ſtrangers to my intention of
fighting my own regiment as colonel; or,
ſhould its deſtination not admit the honour of
meeting the enemy in that capacity, of offer-
ing myſelf as a volunteer in the ranks of any
corps that might be more fortunately ſituated.

Theſe ſeveral feelings, and many others in-
cident to an oppreſſed man, were doubtleſs
duly conſidered; for at the criſis when they
could operate moſt forcibly, it was thought
proper moſt to inſult me; at the criſis when
the King's ſervants openly announced, that
not a ſhip or a ſoldier could be ſpared from our
inter-

internal defence, a fentence of banifhment was fent me, and even that not in an order, but a reprimand—a fubmiffion to ignominy was required of me; for to put me wholly out of a capacity to draw my fword at fuch a moment, was virtually, in point of difgrace, to break it over my head. My enemies might have fpared fuperfluous provocations. This alone would have fufficed to prove their fagacity, and to effect their purpofe. Let it not be fuppofed they want knowledge of the human heart. There are among them, who can difcern its receffes, and have the fkill and the triumph to make a foldier's honour and fenfibility the inftiuments of his own deftruction

I could no longer brook the treatment I received. My letter, of the 9th October to the Secretary at War, [*App. No. 5*] contains my general fentiments. I fhall now proceed to ftate to you, the principles of my parliamentary conduct fince my return from America, for which I hold myfelf peculiarly and ftrictly accountable to you, and which I have only poftponed hitherto, to avoid interrupting the relation of my other proceedings.

I am ready to confefs that I have been a determined oppofer of the King's Minifters, but my oppofition has been the caufe and not the confequence of my ill treatment. Severity, ingratitude, or even injuftice, though exercifed againft me in the degree you have feen,

I fhould

I fhould think very infufficient reafons for
fuch a determination. He would ill deferve
the truft of his country in its prefent exigency who could act againft men in public ftation, upon any refentments unconnected with
public wrongs.

Gentlemen, I will take the matter fhort.
If the ftate of the nation, in its wars; in its
negociations; in its concerns with its remaining
colonies; or in the internal policy and government of thefe kingdoms, can afford the fmalleft countenance to an opinion of integrity and
capacity in adminiftration, I am ready to abide
every cenfure for being, what I am, a determined enemy to it. I have been in a fituation
to fee, that in a complicated and alarming war,
when unfupported by any alliances, the kingdom was left folely to its own native military
force, that fole reliance was difcouraged and
depreciated. I faw a fyftematical defign of
vilifying and difgracing every officer whom
thefe Minifters had ever employed by fea or
land; and thofe moft who ftood higheft in the
opinion of their feveral profeffions. The ruin
of officers forms almoft the whole of their military fyftem; and if I have experienced my
full meafure of their hoftility, it only fhews
the extent of their plan; having furnifhed little elfe than my zeal and induftry as a title to
their malevolence.

As to their political plan, its object is to
impofe upon the nation from feffion to fef-

D   fion.

fion. Far from profiting themfelves, or fuf-
fering others to profit by bitter experience,
they exift by bringing forth a fucceffion of deceits. I cannot fhut my eyes againft my own
certain knowledge of fome of the moft fatal
of thefe deceits refpecting America; nor reftrain my juft and natural indignation at their
effects, without forfeiting every feeling for my
country

If this explanation appears warm, be affured
it is the warmth of conviction. Had my fentiments been lefs fincere, my lot would have
been very different.

But, in thefe times when fo little credit is
given to principle in political matters, you
may perhaps be told, that I have been follow-
ing the dictates of party, and deluded by vain
expectations of popularity to facrifice myfelf
to their purfuits. My friends, I am fure,
would treat fuch an imputation with the fame
contempt they do every other illiberal cenfure; but I owe it to truth and propriety to
juftify them. The men with whom I have
the honour to act have no objects, but to
fave their country; if they had, they might
long ago have obtained them, and they would
fcorn to accept, as I fhould to offer, an union
upon any other terms than a participation of
that caufe.

My actions have been the mere refult of my
own fentiments. My refignation in particular
was made upon the impulfe of honour as it
ftruck my own breaft: and why fhould it be
thought

thought ftrange ? I hope that under that in-
fluence alone, I am capable of greater effoits
than any I have made in relinquifhing the liberal accommodations of a life, to which I have
been ufed ; and of retreating into the competence of a very private gentleman. It comes
recommended by the reflection, that after being
entrufted with a confiderable coffer of the ftate,
and other opportunities opened of obtaining
wealth at the undue expence of the public,
my fortune is lefs than it would have been, had
I never ferved in the American war.

It would be very contradictory to my fentiments of your characters to think this avow-
al could be prejudicial to me at Prefton. In
one of the moft violent election contefts
known in England, and in fome refpects the
moft expenfive, the pooreft among the voters,
I mention it equally to the honour of both
parties, were uncorrupted. Should therefore
the integrity of my intentions appear in this
appeal, and the paft independence of my conduct be confidered as a pledge for the future,
I have no fear that the reduction of between
three and four thoufand pounds a year, will
be an obftruction to the honour of ferving
you.

The truft of my country in parliament is
too facred in my fenfe to be renounced, while
I am thought worthy to be continued in it.
As for the other objects which moft intereft
the multitude, and once interefted me, my

D 2   temper

temper oi my misfortunes have made them matters of perfect indifference—My ambition is dead ; my occupation is gone—the humble arrangements of my new ftate are made ; and and my whole profpects or hopes on this fide the grave, concenter in the prefervation of my friendfhips, and the tranquility of my confcience.

I have the honour to be, with the trueft refpect, affection and attachment,

Gentlemen,

your moft obliged,

and moft obedient

humble Servant,

J. BURGOYNE.

Hertford-Street,
Oct. 23, 1779.

APPENDIX,

APPENDIX.

[No. 1.]

Correſpondence with Loɩd Barɩ ington.

SIR,   *War-Office, June* 5, 1779.

The King, judging your preſence materɪal to the troopˏ detaɪned priſoners in New England, undeɩ the convention of Saratoga; and findɪng in a letter of yours to Sɪr Wɪlliam Howe, dated April 9, 1778, " that you " truſt a ſhort tɪme at Bath will enable you " to return to America,*" hɪs Majeſty ɪs pleaſed to order that you ſhall repair to Boſton as ſoon as you have tried the Bath Waters, in the manner you propoſe.

I have the honour to be, SIR,

  Your moſt obedient humble Servant,

Lieut. Gen. Burgoyne, BARRINGTON.
Hertford-Street.

---

* Paragraph of the letter from Lɪeutenat General Burgoyne to Sɪr Wɪllɪam Howe, whɪch was made the foundatɪon of the above condɪtɪonal order.

" I need not expatɪate upon the ſatɪsfaƈtɪon I ſhould feel at " beɪng put agaˈn ɪn a ſɪtuatɪon to ſerve under you, as ſoon " as my health wɪll enable me ——*I truſt that a very ſhort tɪme* " *at Bath wɪll effeƈt that purpoſe.*

" I have only to add, my truſt that you wɪll cor tɪnue to me " the frɪendſhɪp and confidence wɪth whɪch you have alwaˎs " honoured me, and that ˎou wɪll wrɪte to me at full by the " firſt opportunɪty, how I can be employed to ſerve your " vɪews. I have the honour to be, &c."

[No.

[No. 2.]

My Lord,   June 22, 1778.

I HAVE confidered the letter I had the honour to recieve from your Lordſhip on the 5th inſtant, with the attention and reſpect due to an intimation of the King's pleaſure. I have now to requeſt your Lordſhip to lay before his Majeſty a few particulars of my ſituation; and to offer to his royal confideration, with all humility on my part, ſuch of my complaints as admit of repreſentation.

My letter to Sir William Howe, referred to in your Lordſhip's letter, was writ in the fulneſs of zeal to renew my ſervice in arms the enſuing campaign. The ſatisfaction of ſucceeding in that application, would have tended to my recovery, or for a time might have prevented my feeling an ill. Deprived of ſo animating a ſupport, and viſited by new and unexpected anxieties, I have now recourſe only, as far as the mind is concerned, to a clear confcience, perhaps a more tardy, but, I truſt, as efficacious an affiſtance.

The preſent ſeaſon of the year, always favourable to me, gives me the appearance, and indeed, in ſome degree the ſenſation of health. But much care is ſtill wanting to reſtore me to my former ſtate. The remedies preſcribed me are repoſe, regimen of diet, and repeated viſits to Bath: my intention, in confequence, was to remain ſome time in the country, to

repair

repair to Bath for a fhort time next month, and to return thither for a much longer fpace in the more proper feafon, the Autumn. But whatever may be the benefit of all or any part of this plan, I am perfuaded, that to ex-pofe my conftitution to the next American winter, is in probability to doom me to the grave.

That I fhould not hefitate at fuch an alter-native, in circumftances of exigency, I am con-fident the King will admit, when in his grace he fhall recollect how often at his Majefty's call in this war, I have relinquifhed private duties and affection more impulfive upon the heart than any we owe to exiftence. The purpofes intimated for my prefent attendance in Ame-rica, would, I fear, be very different from fervices.

The army I commanded, credulous in my favour, and attached to me by the feries of conflicts and misfortunes we have in common fuftained, would not find material confolation from my return in difgrace; and their difap-pointment could not but be enhanced by fuch an indication, that Government either thought it inexpedient to ratify the convention of Sara-toga, or defpaired of a ratification effectuating the redemption of that army; for they would not conceive it poffible, had the return of the troops been in view, that any perfon would have advifed the King to what then might have appeared fo harfh an act as fending

an

an infirm, calumniated, unheard complainant, across the Atlantic, merely to infpect their embarkation.

Your Lordfhip will perceive the parts of this letter which apply to the council of the throne, from whence I am to fuppofe the order I have recieved originated, and in your juftice and generofity you will guard me, my Lord, from any fuppofable prefumption of expoftulating with the King in perfon. But I apply to the fame qualities in your Lordfhip's mind, for pointing out to his Majefty, independently of his council, other letters, among thofe trarfmitted to the fecretary of ftate, alledging other reafons, and thofe more prevalent than the attention to health for my return to England; and permit me, my Lord, to add, that every one of them receives ten-fold weight from what has happened lately, for my continuance in England. The fpecial reafon upon which I chiefly reft at prefent, my Lord, is a vindication of my honour.

Until that by full and proper trial is cleared to my Sovereign and to my country, I confefs I fhould feel a removal from hence, though enforced by the term duty, the fevereft fentence of exile ever impofed; and when the time and circumftances of fuch removal are farther confidered, that Britain is threatened with invafion, and that after an enemy has fet my arm at liberty, I am forbid a fhare in her defence by the council of

my

my own fovereign—After thefe confiderations, can I, my Lord, be deemed offenfive if I venture to declare that fo marked a combination of difpleafure and hard treatment, would be more than I fhould be able, or perhaps ought to bear.

My caufe, my Lord, thus committed to your office and character, I have only to add my reliance that you will do it juftice, and the refpect with which I have the honour to be, &c. &c. &c.

Lord Barrington.

[No. 3.]

S I R,   *War-Office, June* 27, 1778.

I took the fiift opportunity of laying before the King your letter to me, dated the 22d inftant. His Majefty continues to think your prefence with the troops taken at Saratoga, and ftill detained prifoners in New England, of fo much importance to them, that he has commanded me to acquaint you it is his pleafure, that you return to them as foon as you can, without any rifk of material injury to your health.

I have the honour to be,

     S I R,

         Your moft obedient

            humble Servant,

Lieut. Gen Burgoyne.   BARRINGTON.

        E   *Cor-*

[No. 4.]

War-Office, September 24, 1779.

S I R,

I am commanded by the King to acquaint you, that your not returning to America, and joining the troops, prisoners under the convention of Saratoga, is considered as a neglect of duty, and disobedience of orders, transmitted to you by the Secretary at War, in his letter of 5th June, 1778.

I have the honour to be,

&c. &c. &c.

(Signed) C. JENKINSON.

Lieut. Gen. Burgoyne.

[No. 5.]

Hertford-Street, October 9, 1779.

S I R,

I received your letter acquainting me,
" that my not returning to America, and join-
" ing the troops, prisoners under the conven-
" tion of Saratoga, is considered as a neglect of
" duty and disobedience of orders, transmit-
" ted to me, by the Secretary at War, in his
" letter of 5th June, 1778."

During

During a fervice of more than thirty years, I have been taught by the rewards of two fuc-ceffive Sovereigns, to believe, that my milita-ry conduct was held deferving of more favour-able terms than thofe which are applied to it in the above recital. I have received from his prefent Majefty in particular, repeated and confpicuous teftimonies of diftinction and good opinion : and I fhould have been the moft un-grateful of men, if I had not felt, and uni-formly endeavoured to mark the warmeft and moft dutiful attachment to his perfon, toge-ther with a punctilious perfeverance in the ex-ecution of all his lawful commands.

Under this fenfe of my paft fituation, your letter ftated to be written by the King's com-mand, cannot but affect me moft painfully.

The time in which I am charged with neg-lect of duty, has been employed to vindicate my own honour, the honour of the Britifh troops, and of thofe of his Majefty's allies, under my late command, from the moft bafe and barbarous afperfions, that ever were forged againft innocent men, by malignity fupported by power.

In regard to the fecond charge, I muft firft obferve that there were two letters from the late Secretary at War, upon the fubject of my return to America ; and though you only ftate that of the 5th of June, I conclude it is not meant, that the other of the 27th fhould be fuppreffed, as it is explanatory of the for-mer.

The

The fignification of the King's pleafure therein contained being clearly conditional, and the condition depending upon my own judgment; I am unable to conceive by what poffible conftruction it can be confidered as difobedience, that I have not fulfilled an optional condition ; and I am ready, and defirous to meet the judgment of a proper tribunal upon that, as upon every other part of my conduct.

In the mean time, Sir, I am not told who it is that confiders my taking advantage of my parole for the purpofes I have done, as a neglect of duty, and breach of orders, and has fo reprefented it to his Majefty. But in this ftate of ignorance concerning my enemies, I muft fay, as well from duty to my Sovereign, as from juftice to myfelf, that they who have abufed the confidence of their gracious Mafter, by fuch a grofs mifreprefentation, merit, and I truft will meet with more of his difpleafure, than they wickedly have drawn upon me.

The punifhment implied in the order referred to, you will obferve, Sir, is unufual as well as cruel. Whether the minifters of the crown, can legally order a Britifh fubject into captivity either at home or abroad without trial ; or whether they can compel an officer by virtue of his general military obedience, to deliver himfelf to the prifon of the enemy, without any requifition on their part, is (to fay nothing ftronger of it) matter of ferious doubt.

doubt. On pretence of military obedience,
I am ordered to the only part of the world in
which I can do no military service. An enemy's prifon is not the King's garrifon, nor is
any thing to be done or fuffered there, any
part of an officer's duty; fo far from it that it
implies a direct incapacity for any military
function. What are the military orders I am
to give to men who have no arms to fight,
and no liberty to march? Or by what rule is
my not being in the hands of rebels, under-
ftood to be a neglect of duty to my Sovereign?
Sir, the thing is too evident; thofe who ca-
lumniate my conduct on this account are defirous not of ferving the King, but of in-
fulting me, and of eftablifhing new, dange-
rous, unmilitary and unconftitutional powers
in themfelves.

While a precedent is eftablifhing in my particular cafe, I requeft it may moreover be re-
membered that I am deprived of a court-martial upon my conduct in America, becaufe I
am not fuppofed to be amenable to the juftice
of the kingdom: and the King is told I have
difobeyed his orders, in the very fame breath
that I am ftated not to be accountable to him
by this doctrine it feems fuppofed, that I am
not capable of receiving orders for the purpofes
of public juftice or public fervice, but am
perfectly fubject to all fuch as have a tendency
to my own deftruction.

But it has been fuggefted when no military
duty could be devifed as a ground for this order

der that I might be returned to captivity in a
fort of civil capacity   To comfort my fellow
prifoners by a participation of their fufferings,
and to act as a commiffary to negociate for
them   Could any fufferings of mine alleviate
the fmalleft of theirs, I fhould willingly fubmit to any thing the malice of the prefent minifters could inflict upon me.   But it is equally
injurious to truth and to their honour and hu-
manity, to fuppofe that my perfecution could
make any part of their confolation.   What
confolation could they derive from my junction to the common captivity, only to tell
them that not a name among them is to be
found in the numerous lift of late promotions?
And that the negotiations to be undertaken in
their favour, are to be conducted by the man
who is notorioufly profcribed by the power in
the name of which he is to negotiate? Who
alone of all the officers who have come from
America, has been denied all accefs to the
King?   Cruelly as I and my fellow fufferers
are treated, I can fcarce bring myfelf to wifh,
that they who provide fuch comfort for others
fhould receive it in a fimilar fituation themfelves.

I am forry finally to obferve that the treatment I have experienced, however contradictory in the reafons affigned for the feveral parts
of it, is perfectly uniform in the principle.
They who would not fuffer me to approach the
King's prefence to vindicate myfelf before him;
who

who have held that I cannot have a court-martial to vindicate myfelf to my profeffion ; and who have done all they could do, to prevent me from vindicating myfelf to my country by a parliamentary enquiry ; are now very fyftematically defirous of burying my innocence and their own guilt, in the prifons of the enemy, and of removing, in my perfon, to the other fide of the Atlantic Ocean, the means of renewing parliamentary proceedings which they have reafon to dread.

Thofe extraordinary attempts to opprefs in my perfon the rights of all fubjects, and to pervert every idea of military obedience, by directing it, not to the fervice of the public, but the ruin of officers, juftified me to my own confcience, in the part I took under the conditional order, referred to in your letter. I found the fame inward juftification in requiring in the moft public manner, at the clofe of the late feffion of parliament, a clear, peremptory order, in cafe the minifters perfevered in their intention of refurrendering me to the enemy.

I have received no order; had an order been fent to me framed in any manner that I could have acted upon it confiftently with the exiftence of character ; I might have made a proteft againft the precedent, I might have enquired of you, Sir, by what probable means in the prefent pofture of affairs it was to be executed. But in deference to the King's

3   name,

name, as a military servant, I meant submisfion. Your letter, Sir, instead of an order for my future conduct is an unjust reproach of my past ; for which I humbly implore of his Majesty and firmly demand of his councils, trial by a court-martial. Should that be refused or procrastinated upon the principle formerly adopted, " that in my present situation " no judicature can have cognizance of my " actions ;" I can then consider the purport of your letter, Sir, in no other light than that of a dismission, a dismission as conclusive as any you could have worded in form, and perhaps more poignant. To eat the bread of the Crown however faithfully earned, under a sentence, without appeal, in the name of the King, of neglect of duty and disobedience of orders, is incompatible with my conception of honour ; an interdiction from my country ; a banishment to the only part of the world in which I am disabled from serving that country at the moment of her fate ; and when every other arm, even to the weakest is pressed to her defence ; these circumstances give a critical barbarity to the intentions of the King's advisers, that an English soldier cannot support. Therefore, Sir, I find myself compelled, if not allowed an early trial, or by the King's grace, upon this representation, restored to a capacity of service, through your official channel to request his Majesty, to accept of my resignation of my appointment upon the

Ame-

American ftaff; of the Queen's regiment of light dragoons; and of the government of Fort William, humbly defiring only to referve my rank as lieutenant-general in the army to render me the more clearly amenable to a court-martial hereafter, and to enable me to fulfil my perfonal faith, fhould I be required by the enemy fo to do.

I have the honour to be,

&c.

The Right Honourable Charles Jenkinfon,
   Secretary at War.

[No. 6.]

War-Office, October 15, 1779.

S I R,

I HAVE received your letter of the 9th inftant, wherein after ftating your reafons for objecting to the feveral fteps that have been taken with relation to the orders given for your return to North America, you add that " if you are not allowed an early trial, or if by his Majefty's grace, upon the reprefentations contained in the faid letter, you are not reftored to a capacity of fervice, it is your requeft to his Majefty, that he will be pleafed to accept your refignation of your appointment to the American ftaff, of the Queen's regiment of Light Dragoons, and of the government of Fort

F   Wil-

William; humbly defiring only to referve
your rank of Lieutenant General in the army,
to render you more clearly amenable to courts
martial hereafter, and to enable you to fulfil
your perfonal faith, fhould you be required by
the enemy fo to do.

Having laid your letter before the King,
I am commanded to acquaint you, that for
the reafons fubmitted to his Majefty by the
Board of General Officers, in their report,
dated 23d May, 1778, (which reafons fubfift
in the fame force now as they did at that
time) his Majefty does not think proper that
any part of your conduct fhould be brought
before a military tribunal, fo long as you
fhall continue engaged to re-deliver yourfelf
into the power of Congrefs upon their demand
and due notice being given by them. Nor
does his Majefty think proper, in confequence
of the reprefentations contained in your faid
letter, to reftore you, circumftanced as you
are, to a capacity of fervice. Neither of thefe
requefts can therefore be granted.

I have it farther in command from the King
to acquaint you, that his Majefty confiders
your letter to me as a proof of your determination to perfevere in not obeying his orders,
fignified to you in the Secretary at War's letter of the 5th June, 1778 : and for this reafon, his Majefty is pleafed to accept your
refignation of the command of the Queen's
regiment of Light Dragoons, of the govern-

ment

ment of Fort William, and of your appointment on the American ftaff, allowing you
only to referve the rank of Lieutenant General
in the army, for the purpofes you have ftated.

Lord Barrington's letter of the 27th of
June is confidered as explanatory of the orders
given in his letter of the 5th of that month.

I have the honour to be,

&c.

(Signed) C. JENKINSON.

Lieut. Gen. Burgoyne.

[No. 7.]

Hertford-Street, October 17, 1779.

S I R,

I RECEIVED your letter of the 15th inftant, informing me, that his Majefty had
been pleafed to accept my refignation of my
military employments, and that I am refufed
a court-martial upon that difobedience, for my
perfeverance in which, you tell me my refignation is accepted.

I muft perfift in denying, that I have received any other order, than an order fubject
to my own difcretion.

I muft perfift in my claim to a court-martial.

I apprehend, that if I am not fubject to a
trial for breach of orders, it implies that I am
not fubject to the orders themfelves.

I do

I do not admit that I cannot legally have a court-martial, circumftanced as I am: but thofe who advife his Majefty, affert it, and they are anfwerable for this contradiction between their reafoning and their conduct.

The report of the general officers, I humbly conceive, is erroneous. And the fubfequent appointment of other gentlemen, exactly in my circumftances (with great merit on their part to entitle them to any diftinction) to military employments, fubject to orders, and accountable for the breach of them, is one of the reafons for my conceiving, that the King's advifers do not differ from me in opinion, that the general officers were miftaken.

Thinking it probable, Sir, that this letter may clofe the correfpondence between us, I conclude with the fentiments I have never deviated from in any part of it; and I requeft you to affure his Majefty, with all humility on my part, that though I have reafon to complain heavily of his Majefty's Minifters, my mind is deeply impreffed, as it ever has been, with a fenfe of duty, refpect, and affection to his royal perfon.

I have the honour to be,

&c.

The Right Hon. Charles Jenkinfon,
  Secretary at War.

[No.

[No. 8.]

War Office, October 22, 1779.

SIR,

I HAVE the honour to acknowledge the receipt of your letter, dated the 17th inftant, and to acquaint you, that I took the firft opportunity of laying it before the King.

I have the honour to be,

SIR,

Your moft obedient

humble fervant,

C. JENKINSON.

Lieut. Gen. Burgoyne.

&c. &c. &c.

FINIS.

Speedily will be publifhed,

A STATE of the EXPEDITION from CANADA, as laid before the Houfe of Commons by Lieutenant General *Burgoyne,* and verified by Evidence.

With a Collection of authentic Documents, and an Addition of many Circumftances which were prevented from appearing before the Houfe by the Prorogation of Parliament. Written and Collected by himfelf, and dedicated to the Officers of the Army he commanded.

This Publication has been hitherto poftponed for the Purpofe of inferting feveral Plans explanatory of the Actions, which it has taken a confiderable Time to engrave.

Printed for *J. Almon,* oppofite *Burlington-Houfe, Piccadilly.*

London, November 6, 1779.

On Thurfday, the 25th Inftant, being the Firft Day of the Meeting of Parliament, will be publifhed

A New Morning Newfpaper,

TO BE ENTITLED

The London Courant,

AND

Weftminfter Chronicle.

And to be continued every Day   Price Threepence.

Printed and publifhed by J ALMON, oppofite Burlington-Houfe, Piccadilly

TO THE PUBLIC.

AT the Solicitation of many Perfons of high Rank and Abilities, this Publication is undertaken. The Editors will not pretume to eftimate fo lightly the Judgment of the Public, as to trouble them with any Apology for this Defign Nor is the Plan of a Newfpaper fuch a Novelty as to make a Detail of it neceffary Suffice it, therefore, to fay, that the Plan of the *London Courant* is briefly this——To give the earlieft and trueft Intelligence of every public Tranfaction, to print all fuch Obfervations on public Affairs, political, parliamentary, commercial, military, naval, theatrical, mifcellaneous, &c. &c. as fhall appear interefting or entertaining The Editors will not be lavifh of Promifes the Execution is the proper Recommendation. They only beg Leave to fubmit the *London Courant* to public Examination

THE Affiftance of the Ingenious and the Intelligent is moft humbly requefted. Their Favours will be gratefully received, and properly attended to.

All Letters, Information, Advertifements, and Orders, for this Paper, are defired to be fent to J. ALMON, Bookfeller, oppofite Burlington-houfe, in Piccadilly, London.

CPSIA information can be obtained
at www.ICGtesting.com
Printed in the USA
LVHW082215011122
731932LV00031B/12